WHITE THUNDER

WHITE THUNDER

DANE RUDHYAR

SEED CENTER
PALO ALTO, CALIFORNIA
1976

WHITE THUNDER was originally published and clothbound by hand in 1938 by Hazel Dreis Editions, Santa Fe, New Mexico. This paperback edition, published by SEED CENTER, Box 591-PALO ALTO, CALIFORNIA, is the authorized facsimile of the original book.

ISBN 0-916108-07-4

First printing, August 1976

To G. M. S.

*in remembrance of days of old,
illumined by the radiance of
Californian earth, trees and
skies . . . and in the constant
friendship of the Spirit.*   D. R.

SANTA FE, N. M.
SUMMER   1938

CONTENTS

CONTENTS

CONTENTS

STORM GODS   DANE RUDHYAR

WHITE THUNDER

*Black thunder rolls mightily
shredded by the livid spears
of drunken gods of fury.*

*Black thunder swoops down upon jagged peaks,
crumbling wildly through mountain canyons,
furrowing with fire prairies and meadows,
glad to spread terror amidst the pale-face.*

*Black thunder gurgles elemental laughter
to shock the virgin Earth into submission,
that may be fulfilled the ritual of the spear
and fields may grow roots and vivid progeny
to appease the hunger of god-haunted men.*

△   △   △

White thunder is a paean of deliverance
from the stale boundaries of too conscious sins
mated in murky wars with too tepid virtues.
It is a song of life fervidly surging
from unconscious springs of the eternal Sea.

White thunder is an epic of joy
to stir heroic souls into power
and wrench from them fire to burn themselves,
phoenix, into immortality.

White thunder, it is the you,
it is the I *that are free;*
you and I singing, dancing,
god-torn, ecstatic, mighty - -

lightnings!

PAEAN TO THE GREAT THUNDER

Foul are the fumes of the plains,
and the dirt of men cries to the stars
for the cleansing rain.
The cities are lurid with the oozing of lust.
Greed clamps its monstrous claws
upon hearts widowed of peace.
Minds, oppressed by orgasms of steel
piercing meaningless and sullied skies,
reel with the ruthless clang of machines.
The wanton year takes its pitiless toll
triturating lives as mere chemicals
in the crucible of harrowing days.
Passively the mob falls to slaughter
along the highways of hunger and crime,
jerked from its living death only
by the mock rapture of priapic dreams.

O Fountain of the Living Light
that quenched the thirst of ancient hearts!
Pure electric Fire that shone
on mounts of hoary salvation,
has the time not yet come,
is man not torn enough with his own scourge,
for you to resurrect our weary hearts,
that we may be whole with wholeness greater
from all depths plumbed and conquered?
Illumined heights! Cedars of Lebanon!
Towering clouds burdened with bounteous rain!

Pour, oh! pour your gift of life
upon us of the dark and the sorrowful,
upon our ebbing days that leave no beauty
on sands desolate with meaninglessness.

△   △   △

O passion of the earth!
Folly of wisdom unwise, for centuries mangling
the very source of its living fulness
and raising evil as crops of sanctity.
Folly of negation and renunciation
breeding sin in brains hollowed with learning.
O passion of the earth!
trembling thirst of love, unspent, unfulfilled;
passion of eyes and lips unclosed
by the tenderness of a presence
that holds in its being the vastness of living;
passion of the virgin and the widowed earth
whose fields no longer heave with yellowing fruit;
passion turned upon self in raw devastation
condoned by false saints and fanatic gods...

And now the tides of death are unloosened
through souls reeling with unfilled past.
Now the rhythm of decay sways frantic brains
toppling over dances of nerves acerbated.
The cry of dying swirls under blackened skies,
and avenging hosts swoop upon the tumult
of those hells called the great cities.

[7]

Cleansing fire! Sheets of white ecstasy
that robe the illumined heights!
Precipitation of love that burns
but to renew and to transubstantiate - - -
I call you, ancient Sacrifices,
purgation of flaming death.
Sons of fire! Holy Flames! Magnificent Ones!
Swoop down upon us, Eagles of resurrection!

△   △   △

What can answer to the fanfare of death
save the compassion of the Sons of Light;
save the great, the tender love of those
that are flames and burn with the radiance
of their own sublime eternity?

I bow unto the passion of the Sons of God.
I sing the glory of their hallowed march
into the womb of the Dark.
My words are full with the sacred splendor
of their star-drunken eyes, lashless and steady
with the immensity of nuptial skies
when the Moon is lost in the magic of the Sun.
Their pageant is curving round the human plains
blazing a new fervor afire with God.

[8]

I sing the passion of the Sons of Light.
I sing the passion of the Sons of the Stars.
Resound, ye trumpets of the Everlasting!
Call ye the Immanent and the Powerful,
the Supreme and the Compassionate - - -
whose Name is surging from the inmost depths,
whose Name is awesome and vast,
whose Name rends the earth with passion of fire!
Great Thunder! Great Thunder!
Hear me!

I sing the passion of Thy star-haunted Sons.
I sing their glory, their love, their crucifixion.

△　△　△

O passion of light! bejewelled agonies!
Rending fire that cleaves the heavy hearts
loaded with the abundance of love.
O passion of light drawn into manhood,
compassionate, tender - - -
Beauty lost, yet recovered
through the drama of haunted days - - - .
Love unrelenting, tortured surge
of Infinite, shrunk into wan bodies
begging for liberation from pain
and desire!

O passion of light, storm-darkened,
stifled by its plenitude,
crying to lightning for deliverance,
crying in torrents of yellow, haloing
the summits bare with silence . . .
Break through, releasing fire.
Shatter the dark.
Tear furrows of light
through wombs desolate,
through shrieking minds,
god-widowed and starved.
Sear life into the expectant.
Father forth the unborn.
O Lightning! God-seed! God-frenzy!
Passion of avenging fire!

The hawk of darkness has gripped
the fluttering earth.
Black mesas mount upon the clouds,
towers of fury grimacing at men
scattered by the wild rain.
The wind lashes the canyons tormented
with paroxysms of water.
Red rocks roll into mock thunder
spouting down mad torrents
that shake convulsive walls.
Madness of the earth!
Fatality of death!

O mighty purging of the weak and the soft.
Dark mass of terror before birth.
Holocaust of seed never to be, never to bloom,
lost souls washed away
into the sea, vast, indifferent.

It is the dance of the dying past,
the carnival of lust and memories.
Orgasms of the dying,
moans of reeling minds
chord into a paean to the deliverer,
a paean to the Great Thunder . . .

a paean to the Great Thunder.

△   △   △

God of Fire and of the roaring Dark!
God whose equatorial passion burns
into the earth deserts of loneliness
and of holiness!
God whose voice shatters immensities
into explosion of thunderous awe!
Mighty God of death that is eternal birth - - -
I call your name of glory and power.

Great Thunder! Great Thunder!
Hear me! Hear my call!
Great Thunder!
I summon you, cleansing rain,
rhythm of electric fire,
mighty roars of torn clouds
transpierced with the god-spear!
Great Thunder! God's voice,
God's command, God's anger.
Breaker of shells, shatterer,
avenger, releaser - - -
Oh! take me that am but a man.

And may the lightning pierce my virgin heart.
May the lightning furrow me, burn me,
throw me, panting, into thine infinitude
and thy love...

and thy love.

THUNDER OUT OF THE EARTH

Wrathful and stark rose the storm,
rumbling through the sullen gorges,
slapping the faces of the rocks
with wet sheets of rain.

Massive clouds raged with thunder
snapping fire at the reeling trees.
The frightened beasts ran wildly
racked by elemental fury.

Silent a man stood
serene within his awakened soul,
smiling at the storm unfurling.
His eyes, steady and clear,
searched for the stars.

Potent with onsurging amber
pines rise with pristine strength,
pinioned against hosts of clouds.

Heirs to ages that sunk into death,
heroes that haunt sky-flung heights,
hermetic and sullen, they stand.

Veiled in star-begotten mists,
valiance carved in the gnarled ascent
of valetudinous limbs,

in the raw power that sank
roots rugged and clamped
into the massive rocks of the earth,

they bear witness in stolid silence
to the strenuous and unstilled power
that ever storms up toward sky-gods,

defier of death, scornful of weight,
fearless fire that burns, unflinching
in flaming passion of green everlasting.

MIRRORS

The souls of strong men
are granite cliffs
dull and grey to passers by.

But the sun, pouring
upon their broken rocks
destiny sundered,
finds in them mirrors
that glitter.

SAN JACINTO

The mighty paws of the mountain
rest heavily upon the desert.

Headgeared with snow
the deathless Sphinx watches
the pageant of men blend
with the dance of whirling sands.

The desert cries out its passion
in torments of fragrance.

The warm night
is thick with love and growing.
Water runs through the palm trees
that shiver.
It kisses their roots.
It soothes their thirst - - -
long flowing fingers,
caressing.

Rocks exude heat
with animal tremor.
One feels their blood
beat,
warm, magic blood
that courses,
heated from below
by the sunken Sun.

Dogs bark at the darkness.
They sense its fever,
its abandon.
Presences linger,
soft, demanding...

Winds sigh
moans of intensity.
Stars ache with beauty
through the swooning bamboos.
The teeth of the luscious earth
chatter with cricket shrillness.

The desert is trembling,
bursting,
aghast
with passion.

I have walked through cities, gardens and oases.
I have suffered through births, struggles and passions.
I have pulsated with the beat of the storms.
I have thrown my life open like a womb.
I have sung and sorrowed; I have dreamt and fought.
Every nerve of me has been scarred and blessed.

I face now the desert and the rocks.
They burn with sun. They fever with light.
They are bare and solemn, live with rattling death.
They tower, yet have no scorn.
Though no sound comes from their tortured peace,
with poignancy and love they speak.
Oh, these words they utter
they burn through, they hollow, they soothe.
They are open like eyes
and closed like tombs.
They are fragrant with heat.
They are dull and sullen,
and my heart wilts
before the grandeur of their silences.

Take me, loveless rocks, into your sepulchre
that lives and surges with passion greater
than all the lusciousness of oases.
Take me who have become your peer in barrenness,
whom life has stunned into ecstatic death.

Oh! take me that am but a mortal
and fain would partake of your agelessness!

I have walked through cities, gardens and horizons.
I have suffered through births, loves and the end of
        love.
Let me rest in you with the peace of stone,
that I too might dream endless dreams,
cold by night, burning by day - - -
dreams strong and old,
foundations of new earths.

WALNUTS

The shell crackles
under the feet of Destiny.

Indifferent, the tree looks on.
It has grown so many
of the little green drops!

Life peeled off
the cushioned acridness of flesh,
battered the naked shell
with hunger of Soul.

Will it be nourishment,
strong seed-substance of matured mind ---
or emptiness, failure

and the famished Soul
weeping?

The Sun spatters rubescent agonies
upon the white breasts of onsurging clouds.

The Sun reels with crimson sorrow
into the dark unknown sundered by light,

While erect in solemn awe, the flaming pines
spear with tense might excruciated skies.

I

The sand flows through my fingers...
Each grain had a name
before God.
The powdered dead
have forgotten
ocean deeps.
They that clung to cool rocks
know sun-orgies
that torrefy.
The mob that was
drips through my fingers.

Suddenly the wind soars.
Clouds pollinate the dust
with liquid seed.
Out of throbbing skies
and shells that lived,
new births will occur - - -
sands of ages to come.

II

The desert is great with flowers.
Dunes heave grey-green bushes
that scatter gold
in prodigal nonchalance
over the sands
blushing with verbenas.
Clouds parcel the sky
of hesitant blue.
White butterflies' wings
that had loved the earth
are reborn as primroses
whose fragrance
causes pubescent snakes
to sway.

Each growth is close to the others.
There is no distance
where love suffuses all
with scented relationship.
Spring is love made perfume,
is life made song.
Spring flows, tangible, immanent.
You and I are lost in the fragrance.
Oranges bloom white nuptials.
The buds of date palms,
sharp breasts bursting with future,
moan to men in yearning for pollen.
The desert is great with oases.

III

The earth is fragrant
with the love of men
and the manure of beasts.
One grows flowers - - -
the other, roots.
All is to be used
gratefully
in the ritual of fecundity.

Work ebbs and flows,
rhythmic pageant of muscle strain
and songs.
Mules and youths
consecrate the dirt
which exudes
gratitude.

It sings to heaven,
it sways with living urge
- - - this gratitude of things
made whole.
It vibrates with abundance.
It smells good.
It is all good
. . . even the bugs
which one must kill.

Around this song of work
the desert praises the rain
with living incense.
Clouds answer.
They caress with shadows
the devotee.
They hold a promise :
the water-god - - -
"Drink ye all.
This is my blood." - - -
Cool blood; rich blood; live blood
which grows gardens out of the dead,
which fulfills.

It is a song of fulfillment
and of fragrance.
It is a song of work.
Trees, beasts and men
are choristers
led by the Urge - - -
strong, glowing, divine urge
that brings earth and sky as one,
to chant

Life.

CARMEL TREES

Ascents of trees strained
toward the golden lips of the sky,
passionate urges toward sun-love,
red flames with green pennants
bent for some supreme flight
across the fog of the wailing sea,
my redwoods, be joyful!

For I have torn my passion
from our mother-earth.
Rootless, flaming arrow,
see me, my brothers,
shooting madly into the sun.

△ △ △

The pines weep amber tears
on the tragedy of the dunes
violated by the winds.
Compassionate and tender
they hold the panting flesh
in the embrace of their roots
and cover its nakedness
with the cracking laughter
of their fallen hair.

[28]

Beat upon me, winds of the sea hollows!
I know your passion
and the countless wills of the sea-mob
that destroy the strength of green lives.
I have seen death staring at me
in the mock smiles of the foam.
Rage forth,
twist my trunk and branches,
hollow my skin
with the superb gangrene
of my resistance to you,
forces of the Unsouled!

You shall tear off me
but the very tone of my own self,
tragic song of deliverance.

Sunward
the earth reaches out
in huge dumb spines
nerved in supreme effort
toward consciousness.

Mountain pines,
ancestors of men,
yet inarticulate,
yet unbending,
trunks of nerve force,
flow out in limbs powerful.

Strong is the root
where no brain yet crowns
the invertebrate spines.
Pine-cones herald ganglions to be
and the fruit ultimate,
the Seat of the Soul.

Needles vibrate under the winds,
as nerves under alert fingers.
They catch the sun
shredded into millions of spears
that tremble.

Exquisite sensitiveness
and strength heroic.
Arrow like,
the yellow pines
shoot themselves at God.

Man is born
pine uprooted and made divine.

Cataracts, cataracts of crashing water gales;
Foam explosions;
Hilarious possession of rocks by white lightnings
forcing their might into granite that resists and rebels,
smiles with black teeth of defiance - - - humid teeth
spitting laughter, rainbows and gurgling rocks;
Green hair, sun-beaten pines, moist and hot with
          passionate strain
where cliffs and water meet in rhythms of color;
Glare of lapis skies stiffening into purple cliffs
to blend with meadows punctuated with deer - - -
Yosemite!
Land of upreachings, of pungent flowers and heroic
          stones;
Land of many faces, rock-shadows of tribes
too stoic and proud for our hollow nerves;
Granite strength, cliff ascents, power of immensities,
stay with me!
that I may be hard and vast like you;
that I may face destiny with the stolid grandeur of
          your silence.

Dawn
Trees raise rhythmical arms
with many-leaved fingers
to grasp the strong life-flow
bursting from the jar of sky
shattered by the day.

Noon
The huge trunks slumber, sun-gorged,
with roots relaxed and moist bark,
big beasts satiated and heavy.

Sunset
A strange fervor runs like a chill
under the earth-skin.
Flowers close,
rapturous with perfumes.
The air grows light,
girl dizzy with first love.
Prayers of the soil,
the trees gather
the silent adoration of all lives
and lift green hearts
unto the stars.

PRIESTS

Sheltered in their own past,
the trunks of palms rise
to celebrate
ever higher
the Sun.

It is the mass of autumnal days.
The consecrated trees
officiate in their golden robes,
dropping seeds like hosts
to bless the yearning of the soil.

WHITE PEACE

I am the snow,
vast and white,
warm to the seeds.

I clothe barren trees
with my woman-love;
I cover all pasts,
absorb all miseries.

I am the great Oneness
made of myriad crystal-names
spiritual mother of nature.

Little children
roll upon me,
and are glad.

White tides of snow
heave from star-widowed skies
down upon the earth
great with seed.

Green tides of sap
blown with the fervor of spring
surge from rain-drunkened sod
in passion of sun.

Chiselled by upthrust and storm,
ravaged by strain of earth-passion,
mountain-kings stand,
stolid and defiant.

Giants there were,
fierce with equatorial strength,
star-haunted, abysmal,
men-trunks mighty
stooping to earth
to devastate with love
women's souls.

Lightning-cleft, and raw
from telluric poundings,
Giants still there are,
whose heroic stature
pierces through rock-strata
strewn with raging streams.

Mighty Rebels!
bound in cataclysmic awe
by Fate's tyranny,
my heart stirs at the beat of yours
in kinship of tragic oppression.

Oh, fling your avalanches
at the sultry plains
disgraced by crawling men
and stretch your avenging loins
torrid with cosmic might,
that the earth may witness,
this day as of yore,
the sublime power of wills heroic
untrammelled by gods.

VERNAL DEATH

Spring comes with eiderdown warmth.
The winds give in
with the tepid languor
of a morning couch
luscious with scented flesh.
They envelop with caresses.
They melt you into vague loving,
aimless fingers wandering,
wondering...

One remembers
the loneliness of seeds,
the dark silence
of soil and winter.
Spring fingers
crawl through the dark.
Electric and soft
they caress the seeds
into passion of growth,
conjure roots and stems
that transfix the earth.

They kill the seeds,
the soft lucent hands.
They kill the peace,
the integrity of seeds.
They dispense soft death
with eiderdown warmth.

The song of falling leaves
drips into the golden heart
of chrysanthemums
carried by the clear winds.
The effervescent light sparkles
over the death of all things
intoxicated with beyond.
A new virginity veils the mountains,
white choir lost in the ecstasy
of the divine Host.
The golden chalice of skies
bare of all but translucent space
radiates with consummation.

The desert has forgotten his yellow song
written on moist earth
in memory of the summer.
Deep in my heart, as deep in the soil,
silence grows into winged peace
in expectation of Christmas.

STILL-BIRTH

Torrents of potentiality
cataract down thundering skies
upon the narrow mountain-lake
man-made for power.

Steadily the level rises
swirling waters to become light
for cities god-haunted and tense,
man-made for knowledge.

Upon the dam the waters press
with the dumb and dark insistence
of fate-parturient gravity
man-checked for power.

Concrete reels under the impact
of uncontainable waters.
Dam-free, potentiality spills,
tears in rapture of aimlesness
man-built homes for child.

△   △   △

Under the downrush of God-life
men stand, engines for power, yet
shattered by potentiality
beyond capacity for use.

[42]

That which could have built mastery,
over walls too weak to contain spills
with ecstasy of aimlesness,
' feeling ' uncontrolled and vagrant.

It craves for human homes to flood
with its soft might; it yearns for souls
to sweep off their self-contained rut
with love, leveler of limits :
Love, potentiality unformed - - -
love that whirls through canyons and plains,
flooding with water and with silt
man-made structures which could have used
power.

DECISION

Fire is eating up the hearts of the poplars.
Fire is eating up the hearts of all men
that stand erect and still in this mauve hour
when a world is dying beyond mounts of woe.
Autumnal fire, frost-released, burning
from within, as chills run down the mountains
icons-like with aspens and pines - - -
such a strange wonder, exquisite agony!

Oh, what is greater - - - to stand cloaked
in the dark-green vesture of immortality,
or to flame forth into golden death,
soul-mate of the waning sun?

THUNDER WITHIN THE SOUL

REBELLION

I have called the Fire down upon me.
I have chanted myself into Thunder
and my fists upstrained bear crashing skies.
Laugh with me, O body! pale shadow.
To dare is to conquer.
All the world's powers are here,
take them!

I have called the Fire down upon me.
I have chanted myself into Thunder.
The raging thrusts of the Gods tear me.
But I laugh, O body!
laugh myself God,
shattered perhaps, yet undefeated.

I sundered with love the heart of granites.
They opened to me the merely man.
They took me with them - - - I became their self.
Now as I walk under the sun
all things give way in flatulent ease.
The roads wind on
amidst soft things and jellied humans
caving in with sobs under the life beats.

O my stones hardened by ceaseless heat,
my granites that bear the pounding of storms,
take me back into your silence,
that I may watch with you
the heroic pageant of moments of power!

''I CHARGE YOU---''

When men shall face their destiny like stones
      with powerful indifference;

When men shall have the strength to say ''Yes''
      to the deepest hell
and walk unmoved across depths most desperate
      and evils most absolute;

When they shall assume the burdens of darkness
      and pass joyfully through all stench
because in them abides the deathless fragrance
      of their own Soul;

When they shall forget their own little self,
their little purity and little comfort
and grow tragically into the great serenity,
quintessence of all storms;

When they shall wipe out the horrors of past days,
by facing evil as the elder brother of good,
accepting the dead with the strength of living
and the understanding which is the core of love;

When they shall look beyond to Him
who tore from gods the Fire of Self
and blessed us all with its curse,
bearing in their hearts His Cross and His Glory;

Then, there shall be peace and beauty
      in the lands of men.

Although I long and strive
for goals that are beyond
all strides and passion;
although I wander
through stark sun-widowed paths,
my steps heavied with the nearness of death;
although my voice is raw
with imploration to the Light within,
- - - yet move I not, secure in my Self,
and my steadied heart beats
with the calm evenness of seasons.

Although my words strike
and the breath of the Living God
tears flames from the flint
of my uncontented mind;
although my hands tremble
with the passion of deeds unachieved
and the frenzy of creations
too vast for human skies;
although my thoughts take soaring
through burning ozones
that make them drunken
with the fervor of cosmic ecstasy,
- - - yet leave I not the threshold of peace,
and my roots are deep in the womb of time,
nurtured by the blood of eternity.

TO ONE WHO CAME NEAR...

Had you come to me when I was still ' I '
your head I would have held into my kisses.

Had you come to me when I was still a man
your body I would have loved into my flesh.

Now your eyes are asking everlasting questions
to that which has no name and no self to answer.

Could my boundlessness satisfy the thirst
of your circumference?

Reach, O beloved! toward the Center which is
          your center,
that very Center whence I ceased to be.

There shall be welcome for you and great rejoicing
in that place where once was ' I '.

(to M. R.)

When Love shall come that is total
I shall sit at the door of my self
and bid the god come and bless the house.
I shall not look beyond the halo
that his presence may throw over the threshold.
I shall not wander about the house
nor recount hours that have fled by.
I shall stare, perhaps with strange sadness,
at trees that have grown so straight from the earth,
trees that tremble with light
as my eyes with diffused tears.
I shall bow my head, heavy
with the emotion of beauty,
and smile perhaps lest one misunderstands.

When Love shall come that is total
I shall arise from all my thresholds.
I shall break all remembrances
into fire-wood to illumine the fields.
I shall breathe in light flowing earthward,
that I may become a thing of its realm,
that it may chant the song of my silence.
And I shall lie, bare upon the earth,
begging her welcome me as she welcomes the sun.

[51]

UNDERSTANDING

To understand Life

To understand the Sun's life
throbbing, thinking, loving
beyond the fire and the obvious light;
To understand the dirt's life,
its longing, its avidity, its weight - - -
and be it all . . .
intensely alive, poured
profligately
in all storms;
afire
in all conflagrations,

yet

calm
at the hub of all wheels - - -
understanding
all heavens, all hells,
all summits and all depths - - -

In the fervent living of all,
in the tense conquest of knowledge
made actual,
in the Shivaic dance of birth and death,
in the rhythmic soaring of the Bird of Fire
singing cycles into being,
to be - - -
eternally athirst,
eternal unrest,
godless,

yet

calm
at the hub of all wheels,

understanding.

VIGIL

I stand.
I wait for my companions
to call me unto them.
The city is big.
It roars.
It shakes
with mad cravings.
In my little room
I wait.
I wait for a hand
to stretch itself
toward my solitude,
for a heart
to vibrate,
as day after day
silently
I call.

I am what I am.
I am my truth.
I was born
to be that truth,
to live it,
to herald it.
Amid turmoil and storm
I remain,
my arms outstretched
toward the companions
who might come.

My hands are empty.
The beat of my heart
hurts.
I wait,
my friends!
I wait
for you all.

PRAYER

O Lord! I am bound
into the love of woman,

I am bound
into the fierce love of a woman.

I am bound into joy.
I am bound into torments.

I am bound into being a man,
a mere man of the mere earth.

Lord! Descend thou
into this man,

that man and woman
may know themselves gods.

My own me is dying,
flower killed by the seed.

O world! Pluck the fading leaves.
Grind them into thy mortar of pain.

Their scented tears may bring joy
to a love-lorn heart!

Scorched by fires of desertic love
human plains groan under the passional sun,
panting for darkness soothing and kind.

God that is in myself
and is my Self,
deliver me from the sun!
Deliver me from this light,
heat to the sullen plains!
Inhale me into the radiant snows
that sing the splendor
of the Mountain-Star!

Mighty Star of the summit!
I strain my white body,
a peak through the frozen ether.
My head reaches to thee and is blessed.
With fervor I receive thee as a consecrated host.
Oh, forgive the sins of my burning limbs
that must tread the plains!

The Woman:

    Dreams.... dreams....
    I listen to the melody of dreams
    asinging,
    wrapped in the beat of my heart...
    slow beats, slow, slow...
    coughing blood painfully.

    Dreams.... dreams....
    I follow them, host of clouds,
    goldened by sun-rays,
    then
    hovering, dark as a fir grove.
    Time roams slowly round the grove;
    slides noisily over brown needles.
    O wanderer! let me be you,
    and merge in you,
    and forget! ....

    Dreams.... dreams....
    I am waiting for my baby-Self.
    I fain would swoon.
    My blood wheezes in my ears.
    It is the wind perhaps,
    the great wind of death.
    Is there in me something to die - - -
    or something to love?
    to love... and be lost.

Dreams.... dreams....
Lull my baby-love, heart of mine,
time-beaten drum whose drummer never sleeps.
Lull me.... lull me to love,
my beautiful drum,
dream-haunted, dream-astir.
This is my woman song.
I hum it through the long waiting.
The needle comes and goes,
down, above.
My eyes are lost beyond the window,
waiting perhaps for the dreams...
for the foolish dreams,
for my baby-love to take me.
Lull me to love... Lull me,
tenderly ... oh! tenderly.

The Man:

I have risen above the sea of dreams.
I am moulding dream-clouds with sun-rays.
I am plunging my hands
in the flour of dreams.
I knead it in forms of deeds.

I salute the dreams below.
I radiate my strength upon them.
I bless them and go on, singing,
toning life for all the new births.

I walk firm through the streets of dreams.
I bid men follow me.
I lead them to the Hall of Life,
orchestrate them into my symphony.

Friend!
Let us dance the dream symphony.
Let us weave patterns to give man joy,
our limbs strong with reddening love.

'Tis the dance of Man.
'Tis the rite of birth.
The world is expectant,
calls us to victory.
We shall win over dreams
and win our dreams.
Beauty is a deed,
cup of victory.

Pangs of love! Wounds of love!
I have cried for them to hurt me,
to bruise my tepid soul
and tear open my virginity.
I have bitten my arms for him
to come and leave me
a bleeding hurt of love,
a wounded thing quivering with memories.
I have seen his face pierce the shell of my living.
I have felt his mouth tremble
from words unuttered,
his limbs pulsating with yearnings unquenched.
I have stared at him
poignantly, madly,
so near that his pupils were like wells
dark with his soul that blessed me.

I have withdrawn
I have bid him go
I loved him
I could not hurt him,
bind him ...

Now the light crushes me
with the pressure
of days I might have seen him.
The house chokes me with walls
pressing with the weight of his body
during nights that might have been.
And I gaze at the silence
weaving its death cocoon round my body
that burned,
and cold seeps into me
who might have lived.

THRENODY

O woman, woman in me
why do you sob?

Your lover I have killed.
Your happiness I have thwarted.
I have charged you with the burden of me.
I have tortured you with my restlessness.
I have flung you into the Market-place
as a whore is flung at the male's lust.
I have driven you through Gethsemanes.
I have drawn your blood and drunk.
Your home I have burned,
your children sent away as beggars.
And you and I, we face the silence,
and there is no peace left
save you and I die into that silence.

O woman, woman in me
why do you sob?

Why do I love you still
more than the silence?

COMPASSION

For him that aches with the pangs of wholeness
what is there to be done among the many
but bear tragically their burdens of self
and sink them into the ocean-depth
where waves and crests vanish into vast tides,
ebbs and flows forever, and forever peace...

CHALLENGE

At the strong I fling my strength
that he may match it and overcome me - - -
if he dares.

To the weak I give my love
that he may be mothered and grow man - - -
if he can.

The indifferent I pass by.
He must yet learn to be weak.

A great personality!
people say.

What do they know?

I am a forest of burning trees.
One by one
the sun sets ablaze the trees,
utterances of my Self.
The flame leaps, beautiful,
earth-fire
strained to star-lights.

A forest of burning trees.

The fire exhausted,
black earth
shall kiss the dark night.

My great personality?
burnt...all burnt....
but
fields, immensity of fields,
cut, torn, harrowed,

filled with seed.

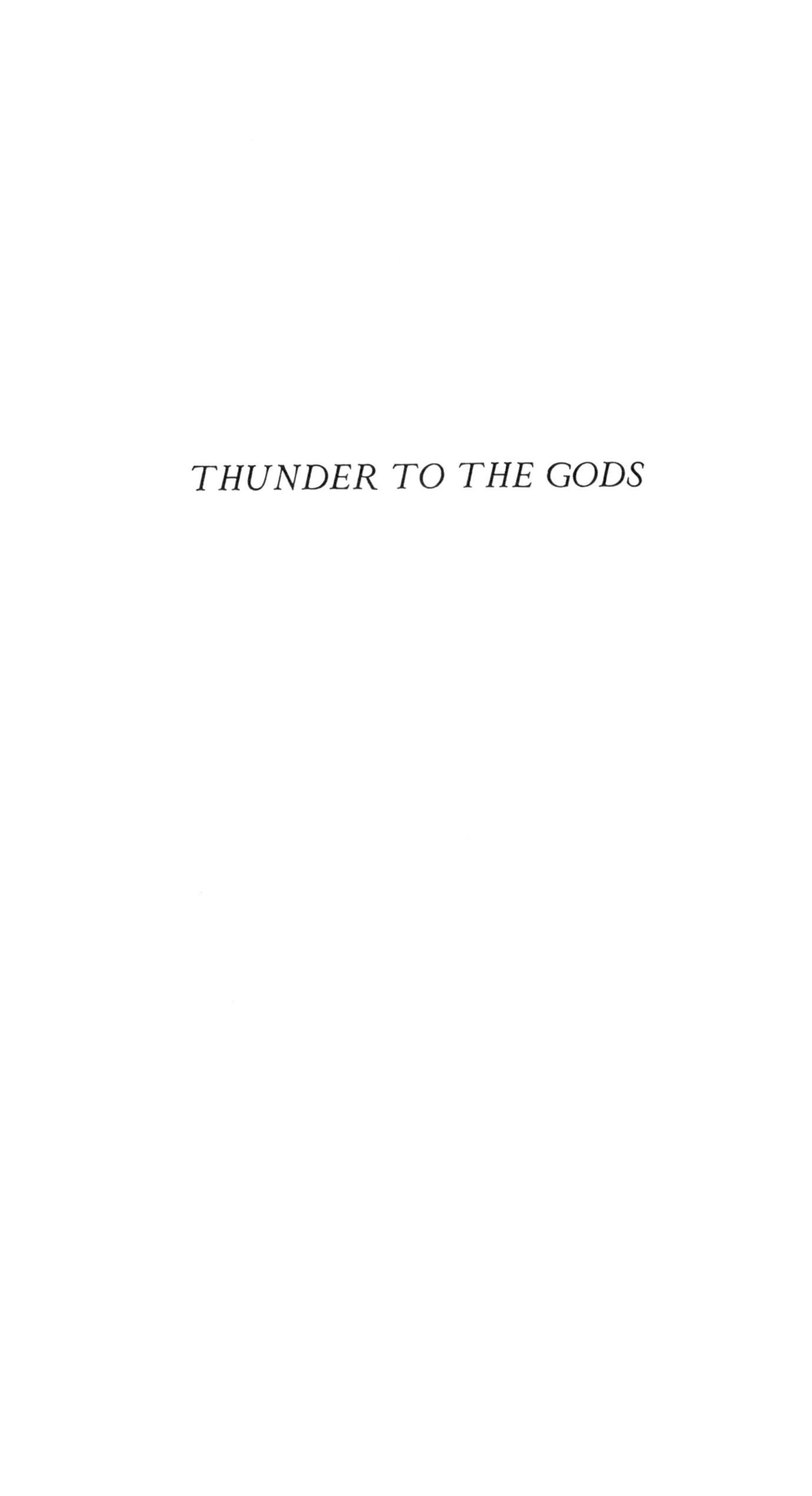

THUNDER TO THE GODS

Rudra! Lord of will and fire, give me strength!
Give me the power to annihilate my littleness!
Give me the ferocity of unbearable love!
I cannot endure.
I tear myself against my racial gaol.
The raw cry of ecstasies sneering at childish selves
furrows me, wounds me
into agonies and strain unbearable.
Am I also but a child babbling words of vain purity,
gushing out self-moods, fake stars on a tinsel stage?
Oh! deliver me from that sham and that maudlin
        pathos,
God of strength and fervor!
That I may stand and stare
with the stoic calmness of men that had power!

Flame of will that tore from the Buddha's heart and
     pierced through the clouds of religious stupor
Flame of daring that drove the reckless Khans across
     the steppes reeling with dying cities that had
     to be cleansed of their human stench
Flame of unbearable yearning for the conquest of gods
     and the ploughing of space, that tamed restless
     minds and fiery horses for adventure across un-
     named realms of Soul and soil

O Flames! Great urges shattering the inertia of man

Rouse in me the power to be, as you, upturned light-
     nings gashing the pall of nature and wrench-
     ing from solid heavens the paeans of mighty
     thunder!

Burn, O silent passionate fervor that tears the
      heart of me.
Like roots of pines swelling out of rocks
they grip in feverish tension,
all fibres of me convulse their rhythm
better to upstrain the devotion of my life-flow.

O Thou that art beyond me the Destiny of me,
I shall will forth thy will,
even unto the death thou preparest me.
I shall go forth into the empty world
raising souls like poppies reddening
on the death-field of loveliness and earth-longings.
I shall call forth the race of heroes
that sleeps in the hearts of rock-men and sea-gull-men
who brave the sea and answer "Yes" to the storm.
I shall make for them a standard painted
with the visions thou bestowest upon me.
I shall clamor out thy tone and thy word
until men and trees are no longer the same
and cycles roll back unto their beginning.

Trust in me, O Master!
whose will I hear beating
into the rhythm of my life-song.
Exalt me with thy command,
that I and thou may more fully commune
into the deeds to be done.
Take me, oh! take me in thine assumption,
Fire that art beyond me the Destiny of me.

And glory thou in that
I shall not falter and not betray thee,
and burn, like thou,
even unto the death thou preparest me.

O Mahadeva! Lord of the Burning Ground,
consume thou me with thy power.
Exalt me by destroying me.
Burn my limitations
into the boundless flame of thy might.
Ravage my heart
with the torrid passion of thy equators.
Scorch my eyes with the fire
of thy own Eye triumpher over forms.
Tear it open, mine Eye. Tear it aflame,
that it may rejoice in the holocaust of names.
Crash open the gates of my sanctuary
and let the tone of me reverberate through space,
thy own boundless wastes,
electric with raging fire.

Lord of the Holy Ones!
Lord of affirmations
whose magnificence soars
with the black wings of endless denials!
Lord of the non-human that is greater manhood . . .
my Master!

I come as an infant light
flickering through the obscure path of thy visitation.
I come with insecure steps and heart bewildered
to give up my search to thy certitude,
my darkness to mould into some strong chalice
where thy flame may burn and thy magnitude condense
for the sake of unborn that crave for electric breath.

Oh! rend thou me into my Pentecost,
tongue of fire that scars
the rich field of the earth.
I will go forth through the wounded plains,
cauterize deeper the gangrene of self.
I will light on all peaks fires of eternal St. John.
And when the day shall have passed
and all men tear aflame
across starless wastes to the void of thee,
then, O Beloved! I shall ascend into thy Nothing,
and rejoice into thine indifference.

I

I shall dance unto the Robe, O King!
I shall dance among the robes
of those that have been born and died not.
I shall plunge my hands into the coffers,
my drunkened hands amidst rubies, emeralds,
amidst turquoises that sing skyward.
I shall draw to myself my daughters the twelve,
the luminous, the rose leaves.
I shall gather them into my dance.
I shall sing to them the sound
that shall burn them into the Robe.
I shall put on the Robe
my Elders have woven,
my tears have washed,
my blood has dyed
into the purple flower of my renouncing.
My hands are full.
My heart is heavy.
My feet are ready.
My steps well assured.
The mountain beckons.
The Sun has not yet set.
Onward to the stars,
O my lonely One!
My child-born, my fair One!
The Betrothen, the Loved One!

[74]

I shall dance unto the Robe, O King!
I shall blend it with my hair.
I shall fold it over my heart.
I shall carry it onward and forever
from sea up to skies,
from skies down to plains;
and northern winds, the frost-biters,
shall not kill the seeds.

Give me the stones, O my Self!
They shall burn with my flame;
they shall laugh with my joy,
and quicken the little children.

I shall light them with my love.
I shall pour out my wine
for the feast of all men.
Open ye, my hands!
Open thou, my heart!
Flow thou, my hair!

Give me the Robe, O King!
I am the Bride,
Thy beautiful dream.

II

Chorus: *Living God! Living God!*

Recitant: "I descend into thee
             as the sun into the flower."

Chorus: *Living God! Living God!*

Recitant: "I enter thy nuptials
             as the bee pollen-heavied."

Chorus: *Living God! Living God!*

Recitant: "I become one with thee
             as light with the leaves."

Chorus: *Living God! Living God!*

Recitant: "I carry thee onward.
             I move thee heavenward.
             I sing thee whole.
             I kiss thee glorious."

Chorus: *Living God! Living God!*

Recitant: "Heed my words.
             Learn my deeds.
             They are strewn
             across spaces.
             They are blossoming
             on the ways of stars."

[76]

Chorus: *Living God! Living God!*

Recitant: "Love my children.
             Comfort my poor.
             Art thou not the mother
             my fatherhood reaches!"

Chorus: *Living God! Living God!*

Recitant: "I have blessed thee.
             I have hallowed thee.
             I took upon me thy heaviness.
             I robbed thee from the sins you loved.
             I made thee rich.
             I made thee empty.
             Receive thou me
             as the Bridegroom!"

Chorus: *Living God! Living God!*

III

Aiyallaha! Aiyallaha!
Surge in me my flame! Surge in me, Fire!

Aiyallaha! Aiyallaha!
Devour the dead! Corrode the still-born!

Aiyallaha! Aiyallaha!
I claim the Power! I am the Will!

Aiyallaha! Aiyallaha!
Raise in me the Living! Raise me from the Dead!

Aiyallaha! Aiyallaha!
I sing the Mother! I sing the blaze!

Aiyallaha! Aiyallaha!
Flame in me, O god shining!
Furrow my flesh, master-toiler!
Sow the seeds of light! Enkindle the Root!

Aiyallaha! Aiyallaha!
The Root is set ablaze! The Root fuses up!
The Root swells into Flame!
Tear the Dark! Tear the Dark!

Aiyallaha! Aiyallaha!
I am born! I AM BORN!

Aiyallaha! Aiyallaha!
AI - - - YA!

[78]

INCANTATION

Strong, strong, strong,
             - - - hear the Soul calling - - -
strong and staunch,
strong and steady,
imperturbable,
stand by me, my man!

Strong, strong, strong,
steel and will
unbreakable,
stallion fire
untamable,
carry me on, my servant!

With power, with power,
             - - - oh! the Soul's cry - - -
with power and prowess
unflinching,
with rapt majesty
unrelenting,
bear forth my message, my man!

With power, with power,
eyes aglow, tense muscles
unyielding,
energy storming on, compact,
unceasing,
furrow forth the field, O plougher!

I am the seed.
I am the life.
I am the future.
I am the unborn.
Father me forth through space.
Mother me on through time.
I am the seed.
I am the tone.
I call from the peaks.
I surge from the deep.

Strong, strong, strong,
I want you,
I crave you.
With power, with power,
I mould you,
I beat you.
Burst forth, image of me.
Clang forth, my gong.

Strong, strong, strong,
ever strong, ever strong, ever strong,
mighty gong!
Infinite strength, indomitable strength,
power irresistible, power inexhaustible, power
        incomprehensible!
I am growing into you. I am bursting into you.
        I am scattering the you that is but you.

Strong, strong, strong,
mighty gong!
Strong, stronger, oh! the strongest!
Ring on! Ring on! Ring on!
Mighty gong!

Mighty ... Gong!

The songs of the gopis ring through the dusk-laden
            plains.
The cup of silence upturns in dreamy hands of Night
who watches from afar the ride of the stars across
the Beloved's realm.

This night He will come.
The hills are pale with forewarning.
The stars quiver and grow faint in awed reverence.

Behold!
The face of Night is glowing with love ineffable.
Its radiance sears the veil of darkness.
Listen to the moon-chant that wells from her heart.
The Beloved has come from beyond the stars.
None shall see Him
but pierces through the stream of the silver song.

Out of the depth of Fire rises He who has no name.
His chariot flames forth with the splendor of noon day
        suns.
Cataracts of light excoriates the path
over which rides the tumult of his red stallions.

His face is like seas of molten gold.
It glows with the incandescence
of vast ice-fields struck by dazzling light.

Agni! Agni! Lord of the ever-burning Heart!
Let me behold thy glory.
Let me bathe in thine ecstasy.
Exalt me beyond the Shining Ones.

Verily thou art the Life of all beings.
Thou singest chants of torrid fervor
in the souls of thy beloved.
Thou art the Mighty and the Effulgent.

I warm my love at the foot-prints of thy coursers.
My eyes glow with the fire they once caught from
        beholding thee.
O Thou, of whom all the worlds are the shadow,
Agni, Lord of gods! Bless my darkness.

He is sitting on his throne of snow.
His body is carved from virgin ice.
His eye scans inward the changing tides...

His passion is scorching death-laden cities.
His breath shatters the walls of man-made temples.
He is pounding the sod with hoofs unrelenting...

Hail, Spirit-born - - - Releaser of matter!
Silence of the above - - - tumult of the below
Compassion absolute - - - passion everlasting.

Hail, O God-seed, sun-drenched, earth-ringed,
ultimate of life, flame of beginnings,
Master of conflicts and identifications.

O Lord! O remember! . . .
Sun of Truth! Dawn of the New Day!
Thou conqueror of darkness!
O Wise One! lead us unto Thee
that we may worship Thee.

O Lord! O remember! . . .
Sun of Love! Brother of Compassion!
Thou binder of the worlds!
O Merciful! descend unto us
that we may dwell in Thee.

O Lord! O remember! . . .
Sun of Radiance! Song of Harmony!
Thou torch of living beauty!
O Perfect One! illumine us
that we may love Thee.

O Lord! O remember! . . .

Mother the Sea
that is deep and boundless,
Mother the Sea
whose tides gave us birth,
Mother the Sea
bless us with thine immensity.

Mother the Moon
that glows with mystic light,
Mother the Moon
in whose heart the earth lay,
Mother the Moon
help us to overcome thee.

Mother Night
all compassing essence,
Mother Night
womb of swaying stars,
Mother Night
upbring us into eternity.

And thou, Mother of Souls,
compassionate and great,
overcomer of fate,
And thou, Mother of Souls,
Buddha Tathagata!
receive us into thy Mystery.

Tie yourself to the Great Man,
tie yourself to Him,
little man.
He is the strong and mighty.
He is the powerful.
He shall upbear you.
His limbs shall be pillars
to sustain your body.
His limbs!
They are pillars of the world-temple.
They are tree-trunks upholding skies.
His power flows through them
trembling under the downrush.
Tie yourself to Him,
little man!
Tie yourself to Him
in love, in silence, in awe,
with mystery of Soul,
with strength of Heart,
with mass of body.
Tie yourself to Him.
Oh! tie yourself to the Great Man.
Tie yourself to Him,
little man,
Tie yourself to Him!

OVERCOMING

Oh! why have you not ears to hear
and eyes to behold open fields of Life?
You cluster like babes in the nursery
scared by the roll of distant thunder
and none of you dare face
the awesome figure of flaming Godhood!
How shall I waken you from your littleness
and from baby smiles of smug contentment?
How shall I force you to stand with exalted power
in the mature glory of your creativeness?
Shatter your mirror-self if you want to be God.
To attain is to dare be that which is You;
alone, despised, unwelcome, divine.
The peace of divinity is in the Soul of him
who has the courage to repudiate God.

*To him that overcometh Me
shall come the riches of eternity.*

Peace to thee! thou that suffer.
The snow of oneness soon will enmantle thy soul.
Wait and smile as days of loneliness
tumble by in weariness file,
brooming with miseries the dust of self
that hid the gold of the Soul-sun.

In the deep and the dark
below the crust of lovelorn things
contented to be but what they are,
see the face mystic of thine Avenger!
Bow before the Rebel, thy Soul.
Bow before Him, the god!
There is no other god, but He.

INVOCATION

Tell the name of the Sun,
tell the name of the Sun,
tell it high and strong,
O render of clouds!
at the face of the dark,
at the face of the weak,
cry it loud
over ranges and cliffs,
over sea and plains
cry it loud,
the name of the Sun.

Tear the heart of the Sun,
tear the heart of the Sun,
tear it wide and deep,
O flame of living urge!
off shallows of self,
off lies of matter,
lift it high and far,
to all men that live,
to all things that suffer,
lift it high and firm,
the heart of the Sun.

Rise, a master of the Sun,
rise, a master of the Sun,
with power and love,
O Self of victory!
Rise from the mire of death.
Rise and sing it loud
to the face of the Earth,
to the face of the gods,
and sing it loud
thy Name of Glory!

Sing Power,
>   *Life cried.*
Sing me that am rhythm.
Sing me that am time.
Sing me, unbounded, inexhaustible,
FREE!

Sing Power,
>   *the Heart hammered.*
Sing the pulse of me, unceasing.
Sing the tone of me, unrelenting.
Sing my red warmth,
heroic fervor that urges men to deeds.

Sing Power,
>   *the Sea rumbled.*
Sing my tides that heave living swarm away from the
>   slime.
Sing my storms that crash upon the solid rocks.
Sing my depths that womb the seed of unending life.

Sing Power,
>   *Fire roared.*
Sing the death that laughs through the core of me.
Sing my dancer-flames with the leaping bodies that
>   love best.
Sing my hissing songs of regeneration.

Be Power,
>   *God thundered.*
I am Power.
I am you Power-filled.
I am the deed that radiates Power.
I am the love that multiplies Power.
I am the thought whence flows forever the tide
>   of Power.

O Power! Power mighty! Power unconstrained!
Power!...
The word bursts and beats
into the flesh of me,
the man.
The tone swells and roars
through the warmth of me,
the man.
It clangs forth. It hollows.
It scatters. It redeems.
I am its impact. I am its fervor.
Its frenzy tears me. Its strength exalts me.
God of Power! God of Fire! God I am!
Burn me whole!
Chant me whole!
Be my Self whole!
>   that I may sing Power,
>   that I may be Power,
>   that I may be MAN,
>   victorious and free.

The world blazes forth in the light of His Presence.
His hands radiate power that upholds cycles.
His smile beckons to lonely stars ploughed with
      darkness.
His love burns, yet it soothes.
His might tears all shells and frees the bound ones.

> *O Beloved, raise thy head*
> *bowed under the weight of men.*

I have seen His face aglow with all the suns of the
      world.
I have felt His breath electric with all the fields of
      Space.
I have touched his hair which flows like comets bend-
      ing with infinity.

> *Rest in me as I am in Him.*
> *Rest in me until your dawn.*
> *For you also shall see His countenance,*
> *you also shall cry unutterable love*
> *gathered like sheep under His mantle.*

He is the great and the mighty.
He is our Peace and Identity.

> *Awaken, arise.*
> *Meet your dawn,*
> *as the earth meets the Sun*
> *with bird songs and heaving of trees.*

Lord! I bless thee
for what thou hast taken from me
and my soul sings of thee
for that which thou lettest me take
from thee.

The powerful taketh and is blessed.
The poor giveth and is thanked.
Hear the sun chanting unending paeans
for that all creation taketh
from his golden bowl
fruits of everlasting life.

" Take of me! Drink of me!
for my Name shall be stamped
upon your spoliations,
for my blood shall surge
in all your children.
I am the wafer and the spring eternal.
Partake of me, men of power!
for thus shall grow upon the barren earth
mine endless seed radiant with golden light!"

Through ridges of moments, sharp-breasted and clean,
eagles of thoughts soar with joyous sun-strides.
In blazes of azure, white wombs of clouds
are great with progeny of flights undaunted.
As the chalice of day bleeds with the passion
of the cosmic Host reverently indrawn
by the parched lips of the Earth's ecstasy,
stars are born by millions, jewels
ringing the mighty hand of the chalice-bearer.

In Him indeed we live and have our being.
Our highest concepts are but dazzling dust
He gathers in His compassionate grasp;
and the waters of space enwombed as clouds
are but soap bubbles His breath has fashioned
for the delight of worlds without end.

Mighty is He, whose smiles are ripples of azure
and whose laughter rings joyously through space
as bouncing streams sparkling with galaxies.

Mother of the world!
I am reaching toward you
and your boundless love
to grow into your giving
and feed my little ones.
My breast is surging
into the expanse of your Milky Ways,
my body deepens to harbor the quest of sailors
longing for the certitude of the stone.
Oh! give me the immensities of your starless spaces,
that I may take refuge
and not grow weary of my baby-suns!

Mother-Earth!
I have poured myself into you with the rain
to seep through your warm flesh
and become rich with the love of your hollows;
and so many seeds have grown this spring
that I am dizzy with the seeing of my face
mirrored back to me by countless lives.
Is there in you, Mother! some deeper abyss
where there lies no seed to be given to,
where there is silence and nothing,
and our still love divinely barren
like the desert?

Powers of the universal Mind
who conceived this form in and through which
I am manifesting wholeness of being,
keep this form whole - - -
keep this form whole.

Powers of all-encompassing Love
who poured their essence into this form
in and through which I am projecting myself
unattached and fulfilled,
keep this form whole - - -
keep this form whole.

Powers of the regenerative Will
who called forth this form in and through which
I am performing the works of wholeness,
keep this form whole - - -
keep this form whole.

O Spring! I greet you.
I greet you with my love,
with the vigor and the fullness of my love.

Spring of the man-woman,
of the love of man-woman,
Spring of the fecundation and germination of all seeds,
Spring of the small year and the great century,
that makes minds burst into solar words
and souls cry out music
that stir hearts athrobbing,
my Spring!
I am swelling into you and you in me.
I am drinking your sap and you my blood.
I am feeling leaves grow out of my hair.
My arms extended brace clouds
and shower rain-blessings.

My Spring!
My seed-gift to the world of Spring!
My seed-love to the need of all earth!
My dedication to the vernal youth
feeling its wings to the New Flower!
My Spring!
My fervor, my drunkenness of Spring!
Exalt me!
Exalt me
to the New Flower!

HERALD

I announce the Solar race of Power-men
who in love have mastered freedom
and in service have proven themselves true.

I announce the race of Prophets and Seers
who having dared to see can refuse to accept
and having fulfilled have right to tear ... up.

I announce the race of blue-souled Men,
who, in nobility proven, shall set their standards
and compel the nations to accept their Laws.

Shall I claim Soul-ancestry?
In the Name of Him that sent me
I announce the coming of the Law-Givers.

Man advances!
I see him holding against the current.
I see him standing, erect.
I see him gaining, inch by inch, over Time
and the down-rush of the Age.

Gushingly, the dark waters of Kali
whirl darkness, decay and death
round his breath which pants.
Twigs, leaves, grass entwine his legs;
the eddied slime suck down his feet.
Cold, cold, the stream rushes on.
Cold, cold, gales torture his face.

Yet I see Man advance.
I see him staring at the summit up-stream.
His iron hands paddle, breaking the flow.
His feet dig down to the rock and withstand.
Cold has no power over the red of blood.

Against the stream craving for the sea-death,
against the decay of leaves that yearn for the soil,
against the water-love rushing to abysmal depths,
strong, metallic, afire,
Man advances.
Yea!
on and on . . . . ever on!